Better Homes and Gardens®

WATER WONDERS

Inside You'll Find...

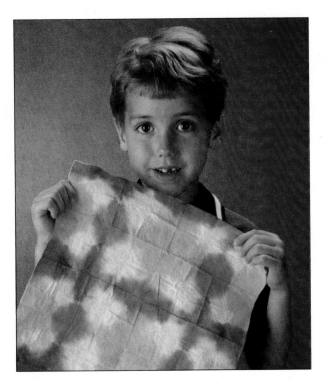

Rainy Day

A mud puddle maze leads the way to the rainbow.

It's raining and Max has put on his slicker and boots for a rainy-day walk. He likes it when the raindrops splash on his face. Can you help him follow the path to the rainbow?

Did you know...

● Rain falls to earth from the sky when clouds become cool and heavy with water.
● If the clouds get very cold, then the rain freezes and falls to earth as pieces of snow or ice.
● Sometimes rain falls in big, fat droplets. And sometimes it falls in small droplets.
● A rainbow forms when the sunlight shines through raindrops.

When the light hits the raindrops, the light bursts into colors.
● A rainbow has 7 colors—red, orange, yellow, green, blue, indigo (dark grayish blue), and violet.
● A rainbow usually appears when the rainstorm is almost over. You can see a rainbow when it's still raining and the sun is shining at the same time.

Can you draw a pretty rainbow?

5

Squeeze colorful gelatin in a sealed plastic bag into a "rainbow."

Bag Me a Rainbow

Have you ever seen a rainbow appear after a rain shower? Rainbows have beautiful colors. You can squoosh, squish, and mush this colorful gooey mixture into a pretty rainbow.

What you'll need...

- One 1-quart heavy-duty sealable plastic bag
- Spoon
- Rainbow Goop (see page 30)
- Masking tape

1 Open the plastic bag. Use a spoon to put all 3 colors of the Rainbow Goop inside the plastic bag.

2 Close the bag. Now open it just a little and push out all the air. Close the bag again. Seal the top with masking tape.

Now, squeeze the bag to mix the colors into a beautiful rainbow.

Squishy Delight

It's time to squeeze a
rainbow! With both hands,
squeeze the plastic bag.

Watch how the pretty
colors mix together and
new colors appear—yellow
and red make orange,
yellow and blue make
green, and blue and red
make purple. What are the
colors in your bag?

A simple-to-make cake that's moist and chocolaty.

Mud-Pie Cake

Have you ever made a mud pie and "baked" it in the sun? This yummy chocolate cake looks like mud, but it bakes in the oven.

What you'll need...

- Cooking equipment (see tip on page 9)
- 1½ cups all-purpose flour
- 1 cup sugar
- ¼ cup unsweetened cocoa powder
- 1 teaspoon baking soda
- ½ teaspoon salt
- ⅓ cup cooking oil
- 1 tablespoon vinegar
- 1 teaspoon vanilla
- 1 cup water

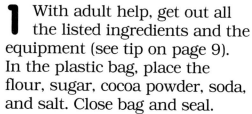

1 With adult help, get out all the listed ingredients and the equipment (see tip on page 9). In the plastic bag, place the flour, sugar, cocoa powder, soda, and salt. Close bag and seal.

Shake to mix well. Put the flour mixture into an ungreased 8x8x2-inch baking pan.

2 Use a table fork to make a hole in the middle of the flour mixture.

In the 1-cup liquid-measuring cup, measure the oil. Add the vinegar and vanilla. Pour the oil mixture into the hole.

In same measuring cup, measure the water. Pour the water into the hole.

3 Use a table fork to stir together all ingredients.

With adult help, bake in a 350° oven for 40 to 45 minutes. Use the hot pads to remove the baking pan from the oven. Cool in the pan on the wire cooling rack. If desired, top a piece of cake with a scoop of vanilla ice cream, chocolate syrup, and a maraschino cherry. Seves 12.

Hints for the Cook

Before you prepare Mud-Pie Cake or any other recipe, you should:
● First, wash your hands with soap and water. Dry your hands well.

● Then, make sure you have all the ingredients needed to fix the recipe.
● Last, get out all the cooking equipment for recipe (see below).

1-cup liquid-measuring cup

Dry-measuring cups

1-gallon heavy-duty sealable plastic bag

8x8x2-inch baking pan

Wire cooling rack

Measuring spoons

Table fork

Hot pads

Wet paper towels and food coloring create a project that looks like batik.

Drip-Dry Pictures

Did you know that you can make a beautiful picture with a paper towel? It's so much fun. Dunk the paper towel into colored water. Wow—watch it change into a masterpiece!

What you'll need...

- Water
- 4 jar lids or small custard cups
- 1 large bowl
- Food coloring
- White paper towel or paper dinner napkin
- 1 large paper sack

1 Pour some water into each of the 4 jar lids. Add about 10 drops of 1 color of food coloring to each lid of water.

2 Fold the paper towel into several layers. Thoroughly dampen the folded paper towel in the large bowl with the clear water. Squeeze out most of the water (see photo). Flaten the towel, keeping it folded.

3 Dip 1 corner into 1 of the colors. Watch as the colored water soaks into the paper towel.

Repeat with the 3 remaining corners and 3 colors. Carefully unfold the wet paper towel. Lay it on the paper sack. Let dry.

Artist at Work

You can create paper towel masterpieces with any colors you like. Then, when your artwork dries, hang it in a window. It also makes pretty wrapping paper for a small present. Or, use the artwork to fix popcorn bundles for a party. Place popped corn in the middle of the paper towel. Then bring ends up and tie top.

Water Play

Max and his best friend, Elliot, are outside blowing lots of bubbles. Max knows the secret to making big bubbles—just blow gently! Can you find the 10 objects hidden in the bubbles?

Did you know...

● Water has been on our planet earth for a long, long time. It was even here before the dinosaurs.

● Water is everywhere. It fills our streams, rivers, ponds, lakes, and oceans. Some water seeps into the ground. It's in the air. Water is in your food. It's in trees and plants. Water is even in you!

● You need clean water every day. Water is used for drinking, brushing your teeth, taking a bath, preparing food, washing clothes, and cleaning the dishes. Can you think of other uses for water?

● Animals and plants get thirsty just like you do. They need water to stay healthy, too.

Make a bubble pipe out of an empty margarine container.

Bubbling Bubble Machine

Do you like blowing bubbles? How big a bubble can you make?
Invite your friends over and let each one make this wonderful
bubble machine. It works great! You'll have bubbles galore.

What you'll need...

- Paring knife or crafts knife
- 1 empty margarine tub container
- Drinking straw
- ½ cup water
- 1 tablespoon liquid soap

1 With adult help, cut a small round hole in one side of the margarine lid for the bubbles to come out. Then, cut a small X on the opposite side for the straw to fit into.

2 Add the water and liquid soap to the margarine tub. With straw, stir to mix well. Put the lid on.
  Place the straw into the X. Blow through the straw to make bubbles.

Max always remembers to blow through the straw. So, boys and girls, *DO NOT* suck or you'll taste the soapy bubble solution!

The Bubbliest Bubblers

What makes the best container for blowing bubbles? A margarine tub works great, but you might not have one around your house.

Take a look at the containers we show here. Which one of them would you like to use? Can you think of any good bubblers?

Plastic soft drink bottle

Soft drink cup with lid

Milk carton

Juice box

Drinking glass with foil

Sprout a lush indoor garden using birdseed.

Half-Pint Garden

Max likes planting seeds in a tiny garden. He always makes sure his plants have enough water to grow green and tall.

What you'll need...

- 1 empty half-pint milk or juice carton
- Scissors
- One 2½x12-inch piece construction paper
- Tape
- Crayons or markers
- Potting soil
- Parakeet or budgie seed
- Water

1 Thoroughly rinse out carton. Open unopened flap of carton. With adult help and working from the opened end of carton, use scissors to cut down 2 opposite corners just to ridge. Then, 1 side at a time, fold top inside the carton. Cover the outside of carton with piece of construction paper. Fasten with tape (see photo).

2 Use crayons to draw a face on the side of your paper-covered carton any way you like.

3 Fill the carton with potting soil. Add enough water to make thick mud. Sprinkle the parakeet seed on top of the soil (see photo).

Place your garden near a sunny window. Water your garden when it's almost dry.

In a few days, your seeds will sprout. Within 2 to 3 weeks, your garden will need a haircut.

Half-Pint Haircuts

Make your garden look special by giving it a crazy-looking haircut.

Use your scissors to snip the green "hair" straight across the top. Or, trim it into a point.

Each time your garden's "hair" grows back, you can give it a new look with a different haircut.

Learn all about frogs, and play a match-the-frogs game.

Splish, Splash

Max enjoys searching for frogs in ponds. One frog is smiling at him. Where is the other frog that matches the one looking at Max? Can you point to the other frogs that look alike?

Did you know...

- Frogs like the water. That is where they lay their eggs. The eggs hatch into little tadpoles. The tadpoles look more like tiny fish than frogs when they are born.
- Tadpoles live in the water and become good swimmers, because each tadpole is born with a tail.
- After awhile, the tadpoles each grow 2 back legs and 2 front legs. The tadpoles' tails get shorter as they get older and turn into frogs.

- When the weather becomes cold, frogs sleep underground. This is how the frogs hibernate (HY-bur-nate). Can you say that?
- To eat, frogs use their long tongues to catch insects. And guess what. Frogs will only eat insects that are moving.
- Frogs make funny sounds with their throats. This is called croaking (CROK-ing). Pretend you're a frog. Can you croak like a frog?

Learning the art of paper folding is fun for everyone.

Paper Boat

"Ahoy there, mate!" Max likes to pretend he's the captain of a ship. He makes a boat that floats by folding a piece of paper. Cast off with your own paper boat.

What you'll need...

- One 8½x11-inch piece of paper
- Water

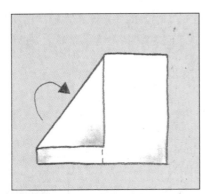

1 Fold the paper in half crosswise.

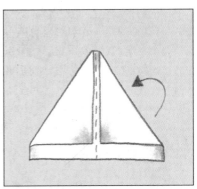

2 Fold 1 of the top corners down to the center.

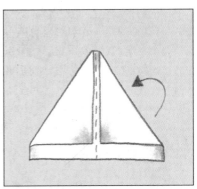

3 Fold down the other corner.

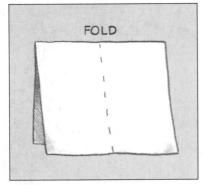

4 Fold both front and back long edges up.

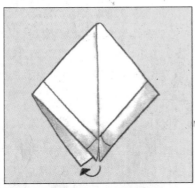

5 Push ends toward the center; flatten.

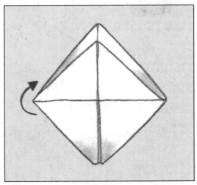

6 Turn bottom corner up. Do other corner.

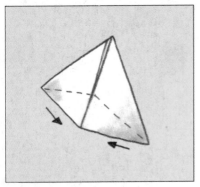

7 Push the ends together again.

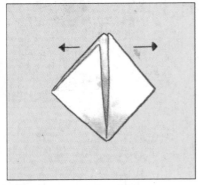

8 Flatten the boat sideways again.

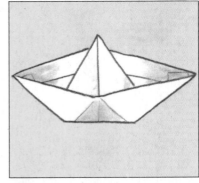

9 Gently pull top corners open. Shape sides of boat. Set boat in water. Give it a push.

Best Boats

The boats that you make yourself are the nicest ones. Do you know why? Because you can decorate them any way you like. Draw on your boat with crayons or markers.

Or, cut out a small paper sail. Tape it to a plastic coffee stirrer or toothpick. Then tape it to your boat.

Sandy

Create a frog by twisting a pipe cleaner around a cork.

Quirky Cork Frog

How would you like having a funny-looking frog swim around in your sink? Tie a piece of string to your cork frog. When you jerk on the string, it will swim through the water.

What you'll need...
- Crayons
- 1 cork
- One 16-inch piece of string
- 1 green pipe cleaner
- Water

1 To make a frog, color the cork with a green crayon. With a black crayon, draw eyes and a mouth on the large end of the cork. (Don't use markers because the color washes off.)

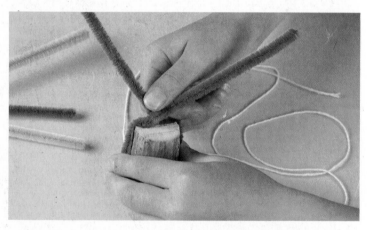

2 Fold the pipe cleaner in half. Tie a piece of string to the middle of the pipe cleaner.

Place the middle of the pipe cleaner in the middle of the large end of the cork. Wrap the pipe cleaner around the sides of the cork and twist tightly behind the small end of the cork (see photo).

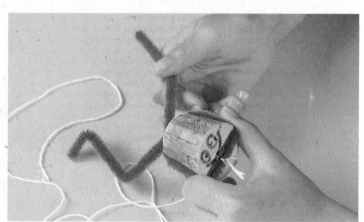

3 Twist the remaining part of the cleaner into the shape of frog legs (see photo).

Float your frog critter in a bathtub, sink, or pan of water. Pull on the string and make your frog swim around.

A special ocean with some unusual items in it.

Deep Blue Sea

Today Max is exploring the ocean. Come join him on his exciting sea dive. Look closely at the picture. There are 6 things that don't belong in the water. Can you find them?

Did you know...

You can do a fun science project with water. All you need is a pan of water and a few small objects. Use the water to try floating and sinking the objects.

Pick any of these objects for your water experiment: rock, toothpick, nail, cork, bottle cap, peanut, paper clip, button, leaf, pencil, sponge, or marble. Which ones can you find at your house?

Some objects will float on water and others will not. Place the objects in the water. What happened to the rock? Did it float or sink to the bottom?

After you have tried each object in the water, sort the objects into 2 groups. Place all the objects that float in one pile and the ones that don't in another. Why do you think some things float and others sink?

A plain paper envelope makes a terrific-looking shark.

Snappy Shark Puppet

Uh oh, Max, watch out! A hungry shark wants to eat lunch. It has big, sharp teeth and it's looking for Max. Would you like to make a paper shark puppet?

What you'll need...
- 1 envelope
- Crayons or markers
- Scissors
- Tape

1 Lick the flap and seal the envelope. With scissors, cut about ½ inch off 1 end of the envelope. On the opposite end of the envelope, draw a triangle for the shark's mouth (see photo).

2 Cut out the triangle. Place the triangle anywhere along the top of the envelope. Fasten with tape.

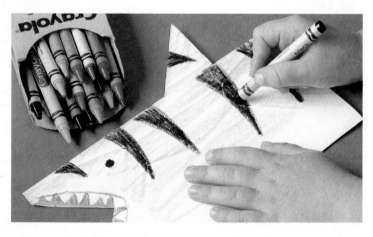

3 Use crayons to decorate the shark (as shown). Draw the shark's teeth and eyes.

To open the shark's mouth, take hold of the top and bottom of mouth and gently push down. Then fold back the teeth edge of the mouth about ½ inch to form the shark's jaws. Put your hand inside and use your fingers to make the shark snap its teeth.

Silly Sharks

Make your shark puppet as silly-looking as you like. For a colorful shark, decorate the envelope with crayons, markers, colored pencils, or paint.

Or, make a sparkly shark by gluing on colorful glitter.

Fashion a lobster, octopus, fish, or other water life from fruit and vegetables.

Sea-Creature Salad

Make believe you're on a thrilling ocean adventure. As you swim around, imagine you see all kinds of water animals. What do they look like? Now make a salad to look like your sea creature.

What you'll need...
- Pear
- Table knife
- Salad plate
- Peach
- Raisins
- Table knife
- Carrot

1 With adult help, cut the pear in half. For the lobster's body, place 1 pear half on the salad plate.

With adult help, cut the peach into slices. For the lobster's tail, place 1 peach slice next to the small end of the pear half (see photo).

2 For the lobster's claws, place 2 more peach slices near the large end of the pear half (see photo).

For the lobster's eyes, add 2 raisins near the top of the large end of the pear half.

3 With adult help, cut the carrot into thin carrot sticks. Decorate the lobster with small pieces of carrot for the antennae (an-TEN-i), mouth, and shell (see photo).

You can also make an octopus' body with a peach half or a fish's body with a pear half. Use raisins and carrot to decorate (see photo on page 29).

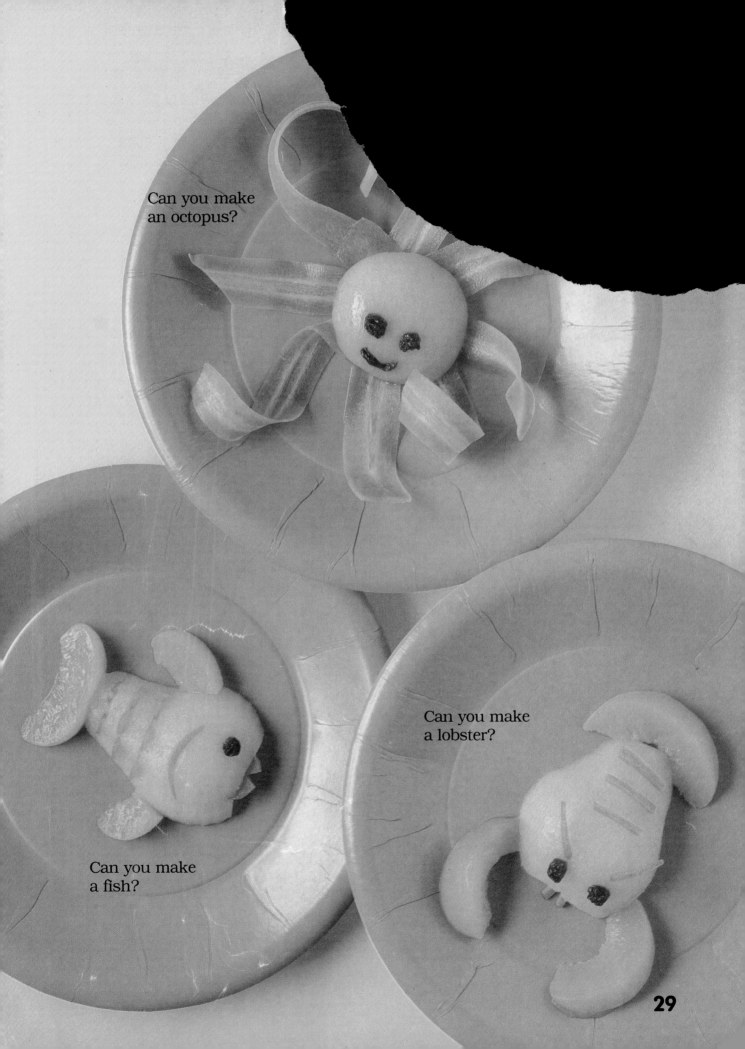

Can you make
an octopus?

Can you make
a lobster?

Can you make
a fish?

29

ages

with more activities,
nts we learned from our
elpful tips.

Rainy Day

See pages 4 and 5

Don't waste a rainy day waiting for the sun to appear. Instead help your children learn and experience a little of Mother Nature in action.

During a thunderstorm, have your children watch for the lightning and listen for the thunder.

Explain that lightning is a quick flash of light that moves from the sky to the ground during a storm.

Tell them thunder is made when the lightning flashes during a rainstorm. And the loudness of the thunder helps us know where the storm is located.

If your children are frightened by storms, your explanations should help lessen their apprehensions.
- Reading suggestions:
Will It Rain?
by Holly Keller
What Makes It Rain?
by Keith Brandt
Rainy Day Together
by Ellen Parsons
The Cloud
by Deborah Kogan Ray

...e a Rainbow

See pages 6 and 7

This colorful gelatin mixture makes a great homemade rainbow. It's quick and easy for you to fix. And your children will enjoy squishing the cold and brightly colored unflavored gelatin together.

For an additional activity, take the Rainbow Goop out of the plastic bag and use it as finger-painting material.

Rainbow Goop

¾ cup water
1 package unflavored gelatin
3 custard cups or bowls
Red, yellow, and blue food coloring

- In a small saucepan stir together water and gelatin. Let stand for 5 minutes to soften the gelatin.
- Cook and stir over low heat about 3 minutes or till gelatin dissolves. Remove from heat.
- Divide the mixture evenly among 3 custard cups (about ¼ cup each). Add 3 to 5 drops red food coloring to 1 of the custard cups. Stir to mix well.
- Repeat with remaining gelatin with yellow and blue food coloring.
- Chill in the refrigerator 5 minutes or till partially set, stirring mixture during chilling. Continue as directed on page 6.
- Reading suggestion:
A Rainbow of My Own
by Don Freeman

Mixing Colors

Children usually are fascinated with mixing paint together to create new colors. Use our recipe for the Rainbow Goop mixture, or paints to let your children combine red and yellow to make orange, yellow and blue to make green, and red and blue to make magenta (reddish purple).

Mud-Pie Cake

See pages 8 and 9

This is a great recipe for a quick-to-fix chocolate cake. It was a hit with both our kid-testers *and* their parents. The parents wanted copies of the recipe to take with them.

Drip-Dry Pictures

See pages 10 and 11

Our kid-testers enjoyed watching colored water seep into their paper towels. Here's another easy water project for your children—creating a water kaleidoscope.

You'll need these items:
● Water
● Small glass jar with a tight lid
● Cooking oil
● Food coloring

Add water to the jar until it's half full. Pour in enough cooking oil to almost fill the jar. Add several drops of food coloring.

Screw the lid on tightly. Let your children shake the jar.

Notice how the oil and water separate into colorful squiggly designs.

Now have them move the jar slowly back and forth. Ask your children what happens to the design.

Water Play

See pages 12 and 13

Children are naturally attracted to water. Playing with a garden hose is so much fun that they may want to spend hours spraying and splashing. Or let them pour water from one container to another to learn about water's characteristics.

Max's bubble pictures on pages 12 and 13 are fun to both look at and talk about with your children. But it also can help them develop visual perception skills. These are important skills for children, and finding the hidden pictures makes learning fun.
● Reading suggestions:
Pete's Puddle
by Joanna Foster
Rain Drop Splash
by Alvin R. Tresselt

Bubbling Bubble Machine

See pages 14 and 15

Bubbles are lots of fun. And, if kids are making bubbles, they're usually giggling, too.

As they're blowing bubbles, ask them if they see rainbows in any of the bubbles. Ask why they think bubbles burst.

If they want to blow small bubbles, let them use an eye dropper. Or, have your children use a baster from your kitchen for bigger bubbles.

Half-Pint Garden

See pages 16 and 17

Watching seeds grow into plants can be exciting—especially if the seeds sprout quickly. That's one reason we chose birdseed for these tiny gardens. The other is it's available at supermarkets. Instead of using dirt for the Half-Pint Garden, you can grow birdseed on a paper towel. Here's how:
● Dampen a paper towel with water. Line a shallow dish with the damp towel, folding it to fit the dish.
● Sprinkle birdseed in a single layer over the paper towel.
● With a plant mister, spray the seeds just enough to wet the paper towel. However, don't let seeds stand in water.

● Place the dish near a sunny window. Keep the paper towel moist by spraying with water every day or so.
● Within 7 to 9 days, the seeds will sprout and start to grow.

Splish, Splash

See pages 18 and 19

Make a big splash! Your children can enjoy lots of other water activities—going on an after-rain walk, having a bath or shower, or going to a swimming pool.

Another idea is to take a nature walk. Go to a river, lake, or pond and look for frogs, turtles, ducks, fish, beavers, or other water animals. Ask your children to pretend they're one of the water animals:
● What does it sound like?
● How does it walk?
● Where does it sleep?
● What does it eat?

Or, you and your children can experience Max's interesting boating adventure by renting a rowboat or paddleboat. Ask your children to point out animals, insects, flowers, or anything they notice while on their boat ride.
● Reading suggestion:
I Can Take a Bath!
by Shigeo Watanabe

Paper Boat

See pages 20 and 21

During kid-testing, we discovered that most of the kids needed to watch an adult make one of these boats before they tried it.

Once they *saw* how to make each fold, they were able to quickly fold their papers the same way. Before long, the children had a whole fleet of paper boats.
● Reading suggestion:
Curious George Rides a Bike
by H. A. Rey

Quirky Cork Frog

See pages 22 and 23

Since pipe cleaners come in so many different colors, it's possible for your children to make a whole rainbow of bathtub toys. Amy, one of our kid-testers, transformed her cork critter into a goldfish. She used orange pipe cleaners to make a tail and fins and an orange crayon to color the cork. Your kids may try red ducks, purple sharks, or pink frogs!

Deep Blue Sea

See pages 24 and 25

Here's a list of the items that don't belong in the water picture on pages 24 and 25: telephone, kite, tricycle, ice cream cone, flowers, teddy bear.
● Reading suggestions:
Blue Sea by Robert Kalan
Beach Days by Ken Robbins

Snappy Shark Puppet

See pages 26 and 27

Show your children the different parts of a shark's body in the illustration below. Then, read these fun facts about sharks to your children.
● Sharks don't have bones. Their bodies are made of cartilage (KAR-tuh-lij). Did you know that your nose is also made of cartilage?
● A shark's teeth are always growing. If a tooth breaks off, another one takes its place.
● The scales on most fish are smooth and shiny, but a shark's scales are rough like sandpaper.
● Sharks have very good noses and find their food by smell.
● Some sharks are small, and others are large; some swim slow and others swim fast. But, no matter how different they are, all sharks are fish.

Sea-Creature Salad

See pages 28 and 29

For these three delicious fruit salads, we made a lobster, an octopus, and a fish by using only four ingredients: peaches, pears, carrots, and a few raisins.

However, bananas, apples, oranges, pineapple slices, grapes, celery, cherry tomatoes, cucumber or zucchini slices, broccoli flowerets, and nuts, such as cashews, pecans, or peanuts, are also nutritious salad ingredients.

Let your children choose three or four different food items and then see how many different sea creatures they can create.
● Reading suggestions:
A First Look at Sharks
    by Millicent Selsam
Hungry Sharks
    by John F. Waters

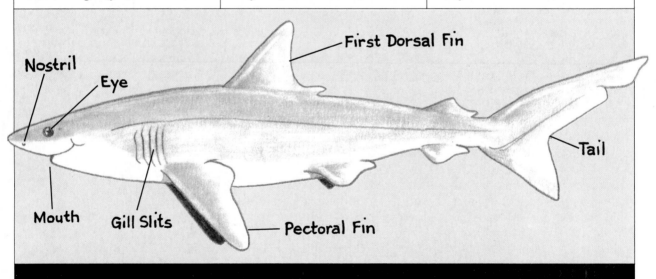

Nostril • Eye • First Dorsal Fin • Tail • Mouth • Gill Slits • Pectoral Fin

BETTER HOMES AND GARDENS® BOOKS
Editor: Gerald M. Knox
Art Director: Ernest Shelton
Managing Editor: David A. Kirchner
Department Head, Food and Family Life: Sharyl Heiken

WATER WONDERS
Editor: Sandra Granseth
Editorial Project Manager: Liz Anderson
Graphic Designers: Linda Ford Vermie and Brian Wignall
Contributing Illustrator: Buck Jones
Contributing Photographer: Scott Little
Project Consultant: Lisa Ann Bielser

Have BETTER HOMES AND GARDENS®
magazine delivered to your door.
For information, write to:
ROBERT AUSTIN
P.O. BOX 4536
DES MOINES, IA. 50336